Jesus Heals the Man at the Pool

John 5:1–18 for children

Written by Lisa M. Clark
Illustrated by Susan Spellman

CONCORDIA PUBLISHING HOUSE • SAINT LOUIS

Hustle, bustle! Crowds and masses
Came to town to celebrate.
People gathered round to worship;
Festivals can be so great!

Jesus and His twelve disciples—
To Jerusalem they came.
At two pools some called Bethesda
Lay the sick, the blind, the lame.

By the waters, people waited,
Thinking they could find relief
From their hurts, their pains, their troubles
Causing them such woe and grief.

People thought that when the water
Stirred and bubbled, the first one
In the water would find healing
And the suff'ring would be done.

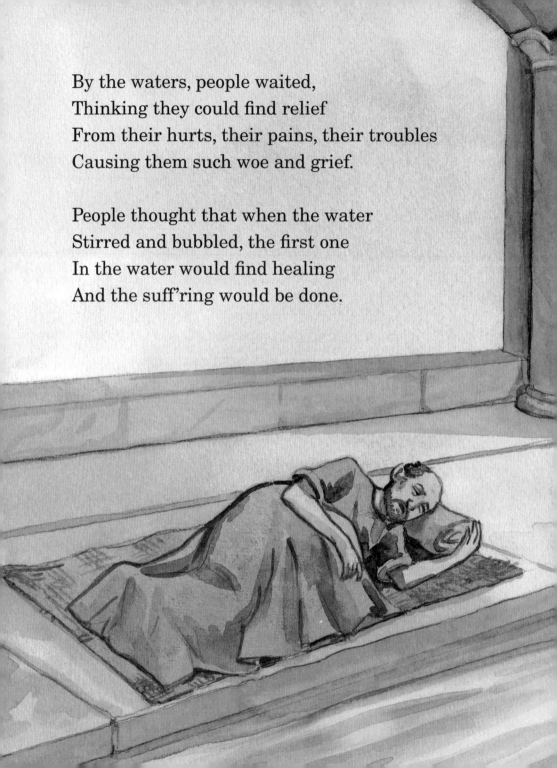

Jesus walked through crowds of people,
Noticing an older man
Who had waited years for healing.
Yes, our Savior had a plan.

"Do you want to be made better?"
Jesus asked the man that day.
Looking past the mighty Jesus,
This poor man began to say:

"I've been waiting by the water,
Watching for a bubble burst.
But with no one here to help me,
Someone always gets in first."

Jesus didn't need the water
Or some chance to come along.
Jesus said to him, "Get up now;
Take your bed; I've made you strong."

Just like that, the man was walking,
Carrying his little load!
Just imagine his rejoicing
As he headed for the road.

But not ev'ryone was happy
When this man passed, mat in hand.
Jews reminded, "It's the Sabbath!
You can't work—that's God's command."

"Don't blame me," the man protested.
"I was told to carry this
By the man who gave me healing.
But I don't know where He is."

Later in the temple, Jesus
Told the man, who moved with ease,
"Sin no more! For that is far worse
Than all pain or strange disease."

Now the man told all the critics
It was Jesus who had healed.
Jesus answered them, "My Father
Works today; I will not yield."

This made those who heard Him angry,
Much more angry than before!
Jesus worked, and now He tells them
God's His Father evermore.

In this Bible passage, we see
People who are very mad:
Those who don't believe that Jesus
Had the power that He had.

Then there is the man made better,
He who didn't know the way.
He was looking to the water;
Not to Jesus did he pray.

But we also see our Savior
Giving health, though undeserved.
He can cleanse our sins and troubles
Through the water, through the Word.

Dear Parent,

This Bible story appeals to us because it is one example of Jesus' miracles. We readily imagine how joyful this man must have felt after nearly forty years of disability. We can understand the surprise of the onlookers as they saw him suddenly stand and walk away. And we turn our criticism toward the Jewish leaders who did not acknowledge Jesus' divinity.

Putting these facts into a larger context helps us fully grasp the wonder of this moment. Laws are in place for a reason; they are used to guide us and keep us safe. To be sure, Jewish law had grown to an unwieldy proportion. In their attempt to earn God's favor, the Jewish leaders had become rigid and restrictive. But God's Law to keep the Sabbath holy means that His people are to set aside time to praise and worship Him alone and not to dedicate themselves to commercial endeavors.

Regarding the man who awaited healing: Just as now, it was customary for people in need of healing to go to the place where healing occurs. Today, we seek treatment at medical facilities. In Jesus' day, people gathered at the Pool of Bethesda, believing the water would heal them. In this story, Jesus did the healing not by water, but by His divinity.

What are we to take away from this Bible story? Man-made laws and medical treatment are put in place for our good, but they are not to supplant God's Law or Christ's healing. God works at *all* times to provide for us and sustain us. There are no restrictions on His provision. Jesus' healing comes to us as His gift; we cannot get it on our own. Jesus comes to us with His forgiveness and mercy, and He reminds us to sin no more.

When you read this book with your child, find a photo of the Pool of Bethesda in a book about the Holy Land or on the Internet. Explain to your child that the pool is a real place and this Bible story is about a real event in human history. Jesus did, indeed, physically heal the man and forgive his sins. Jesus does, indeed, provide us with the same gifts of mercy and love.

The Editor